What Do You Like?

Janine Scott

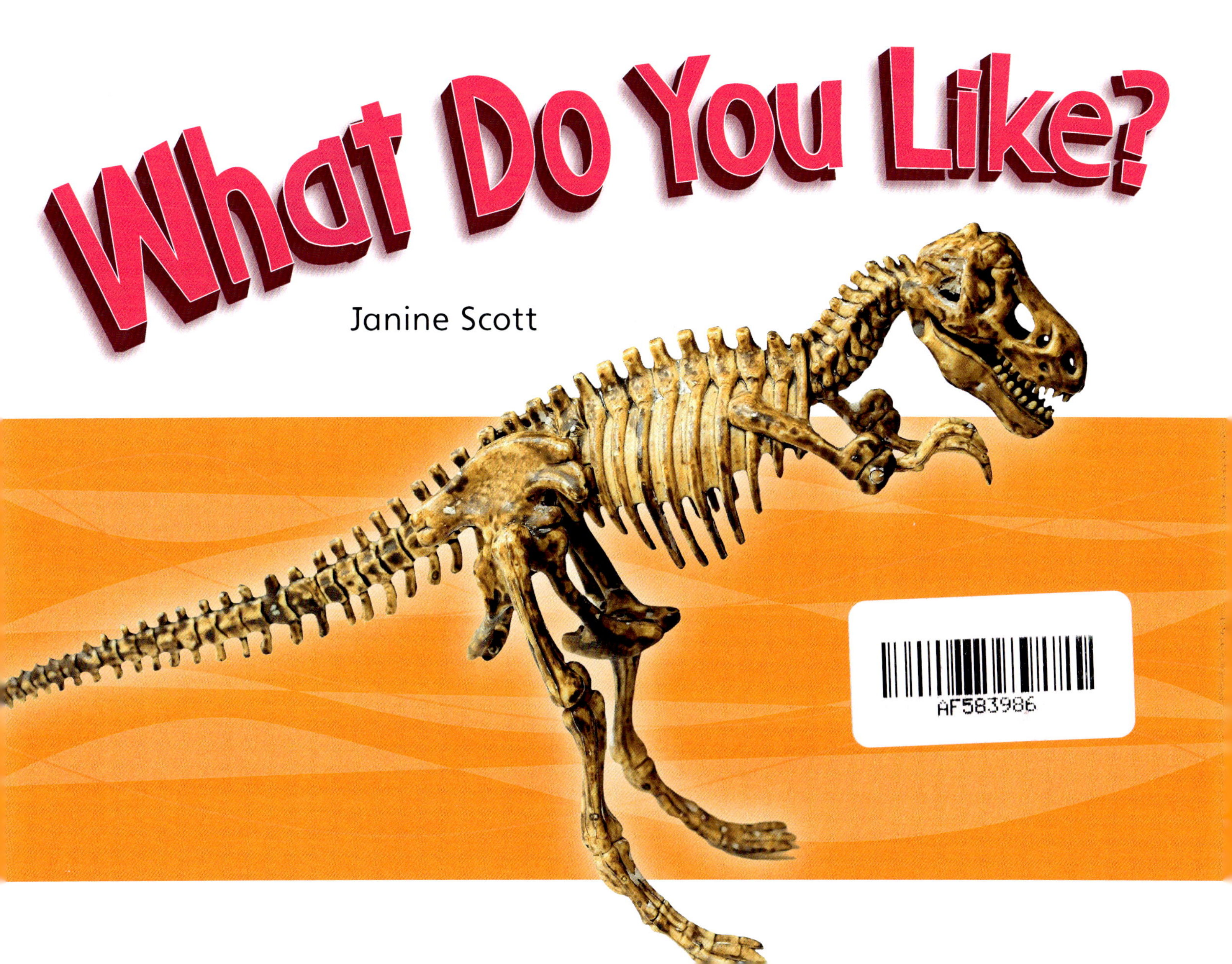

This is a plane.
I like my plane.

This is a kite.
I like my kite.

This is a basketball.
I like my basketball.

This is a dinosaur.
I like my dinosaur.

This is a guitar.
I like my guitar.

This is a teddy bear.
I like my teddy bear.

What do you like?